'Hurry inside!' called Debbie. 'We want to shut the
door so the hall will get nice and cosy.'

To Robert
love Bart & Em

Text by Christina Goodings
Illustrations copyright © 1999 Maxwell Lawrence Dorsey
This edition copyright © 1999 Lion Publishing

The moral rights of the author and illustrator
have been asserted

Published by
Lion Publishing plc
Sandy Lane West, Oxford, England
www.lion-publishing.co.uk
ISBN 0 7459 4047 1 (hardback)
ISBN 0 7459 4192 3 (paperback)
Lion Publishing
4050 Lee Vance View Colorado Springs,
CO 80918, USA
ISBN 0 7459 4047 1

First UK hardback edition 1999
First US hardback edition 2000
10 9 8 7 6 5 4 3 2 1 0
First UK paperback edition 2000
10 9 8 7 6 5 4 3 2 1 0

A catalogue record for this book is available
from the British Library

Library of Congress CIP data applied for

Typeset in 22/37 Baskerville MT Schlbk
Printed and bound in Singapore

Bartimouse

& the Christmas Mystery

Words by Christina Goodings

Pictures by Maxwell Lawrence Dorsey

LION
Children's Books

Once inside, Debbie pulled from her bag a long, thin, brown cushion. She had stitched a face on one end and added big ears. 'This is Door Mouse,' she said. 'Door Mouse is going to lie across the door, to stop cold air blowing into the hall.

'In our cosy hall,' Debbie went on, 'we're going to get ready for Christmas. Today, we're going to make about a million stars. Here's how to draw a star with just five straight lines.'

Everyone worked hard: drawing, colouring, cutting out and adding long strings to their stars. Debbie starting hanging the first hundred stars from the ceiling.

Then everyone gathered round for juice and biscuits, and began to learn some Christmas songs.

Later, as the sky grew dark and the stars began to twinkle, Bartimouse and Emma were still out gathering bits of dried grass to use as stuffing for the cushion they wanted to make.

That evening, they made a long tube of cloth. They stuffed it with the dried grass and tied the ends shut.

By next morning, Bartimouse and Emma were very glad they had made their cosy cushion. Snow had fallen. There was no dried grass to be found.

Inside, Debbie made the room snug and everyone sat round. 'This is the Christmas story,' she said. 'This box is a stable room.'

A *stable* isn't a cosy room.

Debbie had made little people out of tubes of paper.
'Here are Mary and Joseph,' she said.

'One night, they were far from home. They had to shelter in the stable. There Mary had a baby: Jesus.

'There was a manger, where people put hay for the animals to eat. Mary used it as a cradle for Jesus.

'That night, under the stars, shepherds on the nearby hills heard angels singing. The angels said that a special baby had been born: a baby who would show God's love to all the world. The shepherds went to see.

'And afterwards, wise men from
faraway lands came to see the baby.
They brought gifts for him:
gold and frankincense
and myrrh.

'Nowadays at Christmas,' said Debbie, 'people gather round the little scene of the stable. They think of Jesus and the angels and the promise of love. They remember the wise men and they give gifts.'

Someone should have brought a cosy bed for the baby.

Debbie showed the children how to make a tube person and decorate it to look like themselves.

She put all the tube children round the manger.

When she wasn't looking, Bart and Em crept up.

At the end of the afternoon, Bartimouse and Emma walked out of the warm hall, hung with cheerful stars, into the cold night, twinkling with silver stars and silver frost.

They took the only dried grass they could find:
out of their own cushion.

The children were very excited when they saw hay in the manger. Where had it come from? They all wanted to sing a carol Debbie had taught them.

Let's join in and sing with the children!

'Away in a manger, no crib for a bed,

The little Lord Jesus laid down his sweet head.

The stars in the bright sky looked down where he lay,

The little Lord Jesus asleep on the hay.'

Back in their home that night, Bartimouse and Emma felt the cold wind blowing under their door. Then, through the gap, came an envelope. Inside was a card.